Maritime Disasters

Elaine Landau

Watts LIBRARY

Franklin Watts
A Division of Grolier Publishing
New York • London • Hong Kong • Sydney
Danbury, Connecticut

J

For Joshua Garmizo

Note to readers: Definitions for words in **bold** can be found in the Glossary at the back of this book.

Visit Franklin Watts on the Internet at:
http://publishing.grolier.com

Library of Congress Cataloging-in-Publication Data

Landau, Elaine
    Maritime Disasters / by Elaine Landau.
        p.   cm.— (Watts Library)
    Includes bibliographical references and index.
    ISBN: 0-531-20344-1 (lib. bdg.)   0-531-16427-6 (pbk.)
    1. Shipwrecks—Juvenile literature. 2. Marine accidents—Juvenile literature.
I. Title. II. Series.
G525.L34 1999
910.4'52—dc21   98-46910
                                                          CIP
                                                           AC

©1999 Elaine Landau
All rights reserved. Published simultaneously in Canada.
Printed in the United States of America.
1 2 3 4 5 6 7 8 9 10 R 08 07 06 05 04 03 02 01 00 99

Contents

Prologue
Disaster at Sea 5

Chapter One
The *Titanic* 7

Chapter Two
The *Lusitania* 23

Chapter Three
The *Morro Castle* 33

Chapter Four
The *Andrea Doria* 43

52 **Timeline of Maritime Disasters**

54 **Glossary**

57 **To Find Out More**

60 **A Note on Sources**

61 **Index**

TOCKHO

The bow of the **SS Stockholm** *after it plowed into the* **Andrea Doria**

Disaster at Sea

Everyone has heard about natural disasters: hurricanes, floods, tornadoes, earthquakes, or volcanic eruptions that take a tremendous toll on the population and environment. Other types of disasters can be just as devastating. Sometimes these disasters occur because of mistakes made by people. Other tragedies are prevented by the smart and brave actions of other individuals.

This book focuses on disasters that have occurred at sea. Although many such incidents have taken place through the years, the text provides a close-up look at four famous maritime disasters. Were these incidents caused by carelessness, poor judgment, or even criminal **negligence**? In some cases, there are lessons to be learned for the future. Other incidents lead us to question whether human error can ever be avoided entirely.

Overall, these stories are about men and women who demonstrated courage and strength when faced with a life-threatening tragedy. We are left to wonder what we would do if ever faced with a similar fate.

Opposite: The sinking of the Titanic

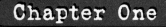
The Titanic

The most luxurious and expensive ocean liner of its day, the *Titanic* was said to be unsinkable. The British White Star Line, the company that owned the vessel, called it "the world's safest liner." The ship's numerous safety features were certainly impressive.

What attracted many of the wealthy, socially prominent passengers on its maiden (first) voyage from Southampton, England, to New York in April 1912 was the ship's splendor. The *Titanic* had a fabulously decorated interior that included a theater, an assortment of restaurants and dining areas, a reading and writing room, barber shop, gym, swimming pool, squash and tennis courts, sun parlors, ballrooms, deluxe **suites**, a miniature golf course, and much more. In fact, the lure of this luxury ocean liner was so strong that many of its first-class passengers had switched their bookings on other ships to sail on the *Titanic*.

Hazards

While the *Titanic* had a great deal to offer, there was something it lacked: sufficient lifeboats for everyone on board. The ship had only enough **lifeboats** to hold 1,178 people, yet there were more than 2,200 individuals on the ship. Through the years, the precise number of people on the *Titanic* has

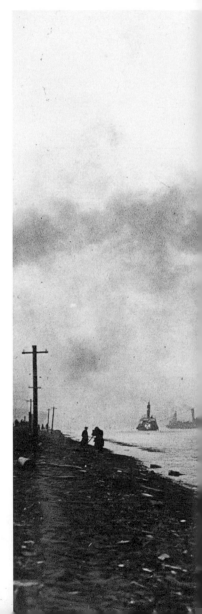

been debated. There was no accurate passenger list, and some historians suspect that the exact number of **immigrant** passengers in **steerage**, or third class, was never obtained. The *Titanic* had also failed to provide its passengers with a lifeboat **drill**, which was customary at the start of most sea voyages. Therefore, if an emergency was to occur, passengers who did not know what to do might panic.

The Titanic *is towed by tugboats from the port of Southampton, England.*

Nevertheless, the first few days of the trip went smoothly. The calm sea allowed Captain Edward J. Smith to move the *Titanic* along at a brisk pace. There had been rumors among both the passengers and staff that Smith and the White Star Line hoped to set a new speed record for crossing the Atlantic Ocean. Smith continued to increase the vessel's pace daily, despite reports of icebergs in the area.

Titanic's captain, Edward J. Smith (right), was considered one of the best by seamen working on White Star Line.

The Iceberg

By Sunday, April 14, the *Titanic* had been notified of iceberg sightings from several ships in its vicinity. At noon, this message had come over the **telegraph**, "Greek steamer *Athenai* reports passing icebergs and large quantities of field ice today." At 9:30 P.M., the ship *Mesaba* warned the *Titanic* of what lay in its path: "Much heavy pack ice and a great number of large icebergs. . . ." For reasons we will never know, Captain Smith did not heed those warnings. He did not reduce the *Titanic*'s speed or put additional crew members on watch.

Then, at 11:35 P.M. on April 14, Seaman Frederick Fleet spotted an iceberg directly in the ship's path. By then it was too late.

Less than a minute later, the *Titanic* scraped against the huge ice floe. At first, the impact didn't seem disastrous—there was only a mild bump and a scratching sound. The collision seemed so slight that some sleeping passengers didn't wake up. First-class passenger Lady Lucille Duff-Gordon described the collision: "[It was] as though someone had drawn a giant finger all along the side of the boat." Laurence Beesley, a science teacher and second-class passenger, noted: "There was nothing more than what seemed to be an extra heave of the engines. . . . no sound of a crash or anything else. . . . no jar that felt like one heavy body meeting another."

Although it did not feel serious at first, the iceberg's damage would prove disastrous to the *Titanic*. Its ten-second collision with the iceberg left a gash beneath the ship's **water line**. Shortly after midnight, flooding had risen to dangerous levels in the crew's quarters. The **watertight compartments** that the ship's owners had claimed would keep the *Titanic* from sinking, were severely damaged.

Lady Duff-Gordon

Lady Duff-Gordon was a shrewd businesswoman and author who started her own dressmaking business after the death of her first husband, James Stuart Wallace. In 1900, she married Sir Cosmo Duff-Gordon, a wealthy partner in her business. The Duff-Gordons both survived the *Titanic* tragedy and were the only passengers to testify at the British Enquiry into the sinking.

The Sinking Begins

Reaction to the collision varied among passengers. Many were unaware of the damage done to the ship or that the *Titanic* was beginning to fill with water. Numerous first-class passengers appeared more concerned about their finances than their own safety. Some crowded into various **pursers**' offices to claim the money and valuables they had left there for safekeeping. The staff had been instructed to deny their requests. Instead, passengers were urged to put their life jackets on and proceed to the boat deck. Unfortunately, some ignored this advice and remained to argue with the pursers.

Other first-class passengers arrived on the deck to face the freezing night air. Some were still in their nightclothes; at least one woman was barefoot. At 12:30 A.M., First Officer William Murdoch began guiding women and children into a lifeboat. Some, still unaware of their dire situation, believed they might be safer on the massive *Titanic* than in a small lifeboat on the Atlantic Ocean. By 12:45 A.M., Murdoch called out, "Are there

William McMaster Murdoch

William McMaster Murdoch was born on February 28, 1873, in Dumfries, Scotland. Murdoch joined the White Star Line as First Officer after sailing on other vessels. At the time of the collision with the iceberg, Murdoch was on the bridge of the *Titanic*. After heroically assisting women and children to safety, he went down with the *Titanic*. His body was never recovered.

This eerie image of one of Titanic's lifeboats was taken by a passenger who disembarked in Southampton, England.

any more ladies before this boat goes?" When nobody responded, he ordered the small craft to be lowered into the sea, carrying less than half of its sixty-five person **capacity.**

Passengers continued to **evacuate** the *Titanic* as the ship's lower compartments filled with water. Though there weren't enough lifeboats for everyone, many boats still left the ship with far fewer people than they could hold. Millionaire John Jacob Astor had helped his pregnant wife into a lifeboat, but he was not permitted to accompany her. At that point, he went to the *Titanic*'s kennel to let their Airedale dog out of its cage so the animal would not have to drown trapped in its cage. Mrs. Astor later reported seeing the dog from her lifeboat, racing about the deck when the ship tilted further down into the water.

By 1:00 A.M., the bow of the sinking vessel plunged beneath the waves. As the seriousness of the situation became increasingly obvious, the mood aboard the ship changed. No longer

Opposite: This diagram shows where Titanic *first made contact with the iceberg.*

Marconi Wires

Submerged shelf of Iceberg

Chart House

Bridge

4 Forward Boats

Boat Deck

4 Stern Boats

Starboard side

1st Point of Contact with Ice

Submerged shelf of Iceberg

Direction of Iceberg after contact

reluctant to enter the lifeboats, people pushed their way into them, gradually tilting the ship to one side from the weight.

Through it all, the band had provided music on the deck, hoping to keep the passengers calm. They had played ragtime tunes as the lifeboats were loaded, but as the last of the lifeboats left the sinking ship, the band switched to religious hymns. The music helped to settle some passengers who believed that if the band was still playing, things couldn't be that bad. When the end was near, the bandleader told the men that they had done their duty and were free to try to save themselves. But not a single musician left the group. Struggling to keep their footing on deck as the ship sank, they continued to play until the end.

There were many who calmly accepted their fate with dignity. Just before the ship sank, millionaire Benjamin Guggenheim and his valet (personal assistant) appeared on deck, dressed in full evening attire. They had left their life jackets and heavy overcoats in their cabins. Guggenheim merely said, "We dressed in our best and are prepared to go down like gentlemen."

Their behavior sharply contrasted with those seized by panic. At 2:20 A.M., the *Titanic's* boilers exploded, sending the ship into an almost upright position. Chilling screams were heard as people slid down the ship's deck into the icy waters of the Atlantic. Numerous passengers leaped into the frigid sea, only to drown or freeze to death. While some of the passengers in lifeboats searched for survivors in the icy water, others quickly rowed away, fearing that their boat might be mobbed by people struggling in the water.

A Final Cry for Help

Through the final hours of the ship's sinking, *Titanic*'s officers had sent out **distress** signals to ships in the area. But the only ship that responded was the *Carpathia*, a vessel under the command of Captain Arthur Rostron. By the time it arrived at 4:10 A.M., the *Titanic* had already sunk. The vessel picked up more than seven hundred people from lifeboats until 8:30 A.M.. The passengers who waited desperately in the water for the rescue ships to arrive, never survived.

Many more might have been saved if another ship (the *Californian*) had come to its aid. The ship was only 10 miles (16 kilometers) from the *Titanic* when the distress calls were

The rescue ship Carpathia

sent. However, the *Californian*'s radio operator had shut off the **wireless** and gone to bed shortly before the *Titanic* hit the iceberg. Although the ship's captain supposedly spotted distress rockets coming from the *Titanic*, he mistakenly thought that the rockets were sent off for a celebration aboard the new ocean liner.

In an inquiry following the *Titanic*'s sinking, the White Star Line was found negligent on several counts. The insufficient

New Safety Features

Following the *Titanic* disaster, several safety measures were created to prevent such a tragedy from occurring again. These included:

1. Creation of the International Ice Patrol to monitor icebergs
2. Use of a separate frequency for distress signals and messages
3. Universal adoption of the distress call, SOS (See pg. 37)
4. Twenty-four-hour radio watch on all ships carrying fifty or more passengers
5. Shifting of shipping lanes farther to the south
6. Requirement that search lights must be carried by all steamships
7. Passenger ships to provide enough lifeboats to hold all passengers on board
8. Lifeboat drills to be conducted by both passengers and crew

lifeboats and unprofessional behavior demonstrated by some of the crew members were cited. It was also noted that the *Titanic* should have decreased its speed after receiving iceberg warnings. Captain Smith and his senior officers never had an opportunity to defend their actions. They rested in watery graves on the Atlantic floor.

Years after the tragedy, the *Titanic* continues to capture the public's attention. Numerous deep-sea expeditions have been

Artifacts found on the **Titanic** *expedition*

made to the sunken vessel, producing hundreds of **artifacts**. Some of the most exciting work was done in the summer of 1998, when an international team of scientists conducted groundbreaking research at the site.

Using new **sonar** technology, scientists were able to create an image of the iceberg's damage to the *Titanic*. What scientists discovered was that the iceberg had not created a 300 foot (91.5 meters) gash, as was previously reported, but six slender slits, measuring no more than 12 square feet (1.1 square meters). The expedition also established a live **fiber-optic** television link on the floor of the ocean. This device allowed television viewers to witness the exploration of the *Titanic* from their homes.

The *Titanic* has long been a popular topic in the entertainment world. Many books have been written about the ocean liner, and it was subject of a 1997 award-winning Broadway musical. While there have been several motion pictures about the ill-fated vessel, the film *Titanic*, released in 1997, won eleven Oscars, including Best Picture. At a cost of more than $200 million, it was the most expensive movie ever made, but it also became the biggest money-maker in movie history. The film gripped people around the world and grossed more than 2 billion dollars in ticket sales.

Opposite: An image of Titanic *resting on the floor of the Atlantic Ocean.*

Leonardo DiCaprio (left) and Kate Winslet (right) starred in Titanic *(1997).*

The **Lusitania** *sets sail on
her final voyage.*

Chapter Two

The *Lusitania*

In the spring of 1915, advertisements in U.S. newspapers warned that sailing on the British ship the *Lusitania* could be dangerous. In these early days of World War I, England and Germany had been fighting for several months. The German Embassy stressed that "travelers sailing in the war zone on ships of Great Britain and her allies . . . do so at their own risk." The 1,906 people on the ship's May 1 trip from New York to Liverpool, England, did not take Germany's threats seriously.

Since the *Lusitania*'s first voyage to New York on September 7, 1907, the

This advertisement ran in several newspapers throughout the United States prior to the disaster.

ship had made more than two hundred **transatlantic** crossings. She was a large ship for her time, weighing more than 31,000 tons, and could travel for days at a speed of nearly 25 **knots**. Most people thought the *Lusitania* was too fast to be targeted by a German submarine. Many were also confident that the Germans would never torpedo a ship carrying unarmed British and American passengers, with innocent women and children aboard. People argued that Germany would not want to draw a powerful country like the United States into the war against them.

The Torpedo

When the *Lusitania* set out to sea on May 1, 1915, it began what would be its last voyage. The trip started off smoothly, but on the afternoon of May 7, the ship came directly within the firing range of a German submarine. At exactly 2:10 P.M., a thirty-two-year-old German commanding naval officer named Walter Schwieger fired a single torpedo at the *Lusitania* from a distance of about 750 yards (686 m). He later said that the *Lusitania* "couldn't have run a better course if it voluntarily intended to come within torpedo range."

One passenger said the torpedo's impact sounded like a "million-ton hammer hitting a steam boiler a hundred feet high." Shortly after, there was a second explosion more powerful than the first, which sent a violent spray of coal, ship debris, and water high above the deck.

The results of the attack were **catastrophic**. On board, passengers screamed in terror as the massive vessel began to sink. Many died when the torpedo hit, while others were left to scramble for lifeboats they couldn't reach in the debris. Some managed to push their way into overly crowded lifeboats only to fall into the sea.

Perhaps the *Lusitania*'s most famous passenger on that voyage was millionaire Alfred G. Vanderbilt, whose heroic

This photo of Walter Schwieger was taken two years after the disaster.

actions were vividly recalled by survivors. Although Vanderbilt was a poor swimmer himself, he spent his last moments putting life jackets on children. "Find all the kiddies you can," he had told his servant who accompanied him on the trip. Unfortunately, both men lost their lives that day.

A Horrible Sight

The *Lusitania* sank rapidly, disappearing beneath the water in just 18 minutes. Floating debris, a mass of lifeboats, struggling swimmers, and corpses could be spotted where the ship went down. Viewing the devastation from his submarine, Walter Schwieger reportedly appeared shocked. He later described the wreckage as "the most horrible sight he had ever seen."

The high number of **casualties** was undeniably chilling.

Although the Lusitania held many lifeboats (as shown), most would not be used to save the passengers.

Woodrow Wilson

Woodrow Wilson was the twenty-eighth president of the United States from 1913 to 1921, serving two terms. It is said that following the *Lusitania* disaster, Wilson was so devastated by the news that he went into seclusion for two days, seeing and talking to no one but his family and White House staff.

Of the 1,906 passengers aboard the *Lusitania*, only 708 survived. Some of the victims were young mothers who clung to their babies as they both drowned. One hundred and twenty-eight Americans died on the *Lusitania*, including a number of prominent citizens and close friends of President Woodrow Wilson.

An Accident?

Over the years, the sinking of the *Lusitania* has raised some important questions. Many believe the true story behind the ship's destruction has never been fully revealed, and that the incident was not as it had appeared. Germany claimed that before the attack, the *Lusitania* was more than just a passenger ship. The Germans argued that the British had secretly outfitted the vessel to carry ammunition, and that the *Lusitania* was actively involved in the war effort.

On her last voyage, the *Lusitania* was carrying **shrapnel** shells, cartridges, barrels of fuel, and military food supplies as part of her cargo. Submarine activity had been reported in the area off the Irish coast. The British cruiser *Juno* was to escort the *Lusitania* through this region, but for some unknown reason, the ship was never sent out to sea as planned, leaving the *Lusitania* on its own.

Many historians questioned why the German vessel had been in the area at all. It was later revealed that German intelligence knew that British military ships would be in the Irish Sea during the first week of May. Some have wondered whether this information was purposely planted so that a ship like the *Lusitania* could be targeted.

The Germans further indicated that the British Admiralty (navy) deliberately allowed the *Lusitania* into dangerous waters, where the ship was likely to be attacked, in order to bring the United States into the war as an ally. The Germans

A Letter to Germany

Following the sinking of the *Lusitania*, President Woodrow Wilson sent a letter to the German government under the signature of Secretary of State William Jennings Bryan:

The sinking of the British passenger steamer Falaba *by a German submarine on March 28, through which Leon C. Thrasher, an American citizen, was drowned; the attack on April 28 on the American vessel* Cushing *by a German aeroplane; the torpedoing on May 1 of the American vessel* Gulflight *by a German submarine, as a result of which two or more American citizens met their death and finally, the torpedoing and sinking of the steamship* Lusitania, *constitute a series of events which the Government of the United States has observed with growing concern, distress, and amazement.*

Winston Churchill (1952)

were never able to prove this, however, and a British court found the German submarine commander guilty in the incident.

The German attack was vigorously condemned in the United States and Great Britain. Former president Theodore Roosevelt labeled the sinking as "an act of piracy." Yet, while the attack on the *Lusitania* has frequently been described as the event that drew the United States into World War I, it was not the truth. The United States entered the war after Germany threatened to "sink all ships, armed or unarmed, in the waters around Britain and France."

Historians further suspected that high-level British officials had wanted the disaster to occur. A letter from former Prime Minister Winston Churchill, who was then First Lord of the British Admiralty, indicated that he supported this theory. In the letter, Churchill cited how crucial it was "to attract neutral shipping to our shores in the hope of especially embroiling the United States with Germany."

Through the years, the British government continued to deny involvement on any level, but for many people doubts still exist. Undersea divers exploring the ship's sunken wreckage have tried to learn more, but the full story behind the *Lusitania*'s destruction remains unknown.

Sixty-six victims of the Lusitania *tragedy are laid to rest.*

The Morro Castle continues to burn after having beached itself.

Chapter Three

The *Morro Castle*

In the 1930s, the *Morro Castle* was a popular, 508-foot (155-m) ocean liner that cruised to tropical destinations. One of its most frequent runs was between New York and Cuba. With no travel **embargo** between the island and the United States, Americans frequently went to Cuba to enjoy the beaches, music, and dazzling nightlife. During prohibition (1920–1930), when the sale of alcoholic beverages was prohibited in the United States, liquor still flowed freely in Cuba,

A modern cruise ship

Oceanliners

Before the introduction of jet-powered aircraft, people relied on oceanliners, often referred to as "passenger ships," for transatlantic travel. Today, these ships are used for the pleasure-cruise trade, or as a shuttle service for overnight ferries between countries.

making the island an even more desirable place for people to go from the United States.

Although the attractive cruise ship with its glistening white **hull** had no trouble attracting passengers, some seamen considered the vessel unlucky and tended to avoid it. Truly, the *Morro Castle* seemed to have had more than its share of ill-fated encounters. At one time, the ship was nearly **run aground**. There had also been several small fires aboard the vessel, which the crew had been able to contain.

Regardless of these mishaps, the ship was always fully booked with passengers. For most of its trips, the *Morro Castle* sailed within five to nine miles of the U.S. eastern seaboard.

Passengers, able to see the beach from their deck chairs, felt secure on board.

Captain's Dinner

On Friday, September 7, 1934, the *Morro Castle* was on its way back to New York from Cuba. The ship's captain was Robert Wilmott, who was not in the best of health. This was the ship's 174th round-trip voyage and the vessel had just survived a severe tropical storm. On the last night of the cruise, passengers eagerly awaited the traditional captain's dinner, an event complete with music, dancing, and colorful party decorations. But Captain Wilmott would not be hosting the evening's festivities. He had been found dead earlier that evening in his cabin, the apparent victim of a heart attack.

Captain Robert Wilmott

With Wilmott dead, Chief William F. Warms (the next officer in the line of duty) would assume command until the ship docked in New York the following day. But Warms might not have been the ideal person for this task. Captain Wilmott had once requested that the officer be removed from the ship's staff because he didn't seem to "know his mind from one minute to another." Another senior officer

Smoke billows from the Morro Castle as passengers attempt to flee the burning vessel.

on the *Morro Castle* agreed, once commenting, "Warms never did anything on his own. All he did was to relay the master's order."

The Fire

With the night's entertainment canceled due to the captain's death, the passengers struggled through a solemn evening. Some remained at the bar in the lounge, but most returned to their cabins. At about 2:45 A.M., a fire mysteriously broke out in a locker in the ship's writing room. The ship's staff feebly tried to put out the blaze, but they could not handle the situation. Unfortunately, the fire spread quickly to other parts of the ship because crew members neglected to shut the fire doors to contain the flames.

The situation worsened when the crew tried to retrieve hoses to put out the fire. The closest fire-hose stations were

Merchant Marine Act

The Merchant Marine is a group of many commercial ships that are private or publicly owned by a nation. After the *Morro Castle* disaster in 1934, laws of the sea were established through the creation of the Merchant Marine Act in 1936. The Act sought to promote the development and maintenance of an adequate, well-balanced United States merchant marine.

out of order, and the three hoses brought down from the boat deck did not have sufficient water power. Meanwhile, thick smoke made it difficult to breathe or see. One ship officer described the smoke as being so dense that "you couldn't see two feet in front of you."

Poor Judgment

Although accounts of what occurred on the burning ship varied among the crew and passengers, most witnesses generally agreed that confusion reigned. It would have been wisest to stop the vessel to fight the fire and prepare the passengers to abandon ship, but acting captain Warms took a different course of action. Rather than stop, he ordered the crew to continue toward New York at a brisk pace. This proved to be a disastrous decision. Strong winds fanned the flames into an unstoppable blaze.

Warms also failed to order the radio operator send out the SOS distress call for help. One of the radio operators repea-

SOS

In 1906, at the Radio Telegraphic Conference held in Berlin, Germany, a distress call was created to achieve a faster, sharper signal. The SOS signal, which meant "Seeking you. Distress!" or, "All stations. Distress!" would be sent in a continuous stream of Morse code dots and dashes (. . . - - - . . .) instead of a sequence of letters. In 1999, an agreement by the United Nations replaced the SOS radio code signal with the Global Maritime Distress and Safety System, which relies on the use of satellites.

Chief Officer William F. Warms

tedly sought permission to send out an SOS, but Warms continued to refuse his requests. More than an hour after the fire broke out, Chief Radio Operator George White Rogers defied Warms and sent the SOS. This would be the only distress signal from the ship that night. Soon afterward, fire engulfed the radio room.

The plight of those on board was further worsened by Warms' delay in sounding the ship's general alarm. Although it was never proven, some passengers remembered that when the ship's alarm was sounded, most of the *Morro Castle*'s crew seemed to take it as a signal to desert the passengers and abandon ship. Therefore, many passengers were left on their own.

Save Yourself!

Dr. Charles Cochrane, a New York surgeon on the *Morro Castle* that night, recalled his experience as well. "Suddenly someone gave me a push and I half fell and half staggered into the lifeboat. There was trouble in launching; it seemed almost a half hour before we were in the water and pulling away from the *Morro Castle*. The front of the ship was a pillar of flame by that time."

Some of the passengers, aided by life jackets, actually swam the 6 miles (10 km) to the Jersey shore. Others made it part of the way and remained in the water until they were later picked up by rescue boats. One woman was in the water for more

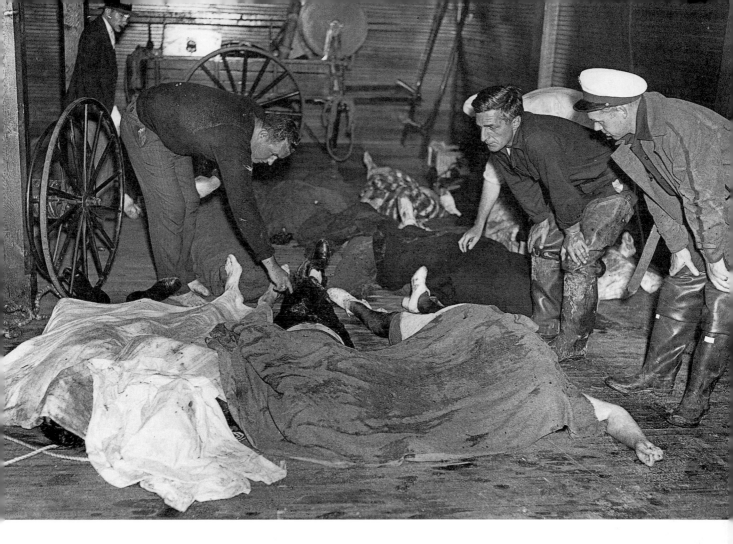

than 7 hours before being rescued. Perhaps the most out-standing swimming feat that night was accomplished by twenty-year-old Antonio Mato, a young Cuban man on the ship's dining-room staff. Mato managed to swim to shore without the aid of a life jacket. Just as he stepped from the surf to the beach, he collapsed, but was soon revived.

The SOS sent out by Chief Radio Operator George White Rogers brought the Coast Guard and nearby area ships to the rescue site. But the *Morro Castle* fire still resulted in a stagger-

Burn Alive or Jump!

Mrs. Robert O. Meisser, a passenger on board, described what she and her husband experienced: "No one woke us. We heard no whistles or fire bells. . . . Some people on deck were crying and shivering in their nightclothes; some were jumping into the dark angry water. Only a few had life preservers. The round ones with the ship's name on them were locked on the bulkheads. . . . We could scarcely breathe. . . . The rails were burning now and the decks. . . . The center of the ship was a mass of flames. The officers and crew did not come to the rear where people were screaming and drowning. . . . It was either burn alive or jump into the ocean."

ing loss of life—134 passengers either burned to death or drowned.

Not surprisingly, many of the survivors claimed that most crew members had acted less than valiantly. One lifeboat was picked up by the Coast Guard holding thirty-one crew members and only one passenger. Of the first ninety-eight people rescued from lifeboats, more than ninety were crew members.

Although the fire's cause was unknown, arson was suspected. Some people believed that an unhappy crew member had started the fire and drugged the captain, causing his heart attack, but this was never proven. A court found the Ward Line (which owned the *Morro Castle*) guilty of gross negligence for not sending out a timely SOS and stopping the ship earlier to put out the fire. The convictions were later reversed on appeal.

The burned-out *Morro Castle* was grounded at the New Jersey shore town of Asbury Park. On the Sunday following the fire, city officials charged 25 cents per person to view the wreck. They collected $2,800 to be distributed to the families of those who died on the ship. To this day, the cause of the *Morro Castle* fire has never been determined.

The Morro Castle as it appeared along the shore of Asbury Park, New Jersey, in 1934.

The **Andrea Doria** *tilts to one side after having been hit by the* Stockholm.

Chapter Four

The Andrea Doria

The *Andrea Doria*, a magnificent Italian luxury liner, sailed for the first time in 1951. Measuring eleven decks high and weighing more than 29,000 tons, the cruise ship offered passengers every fashionable comfort available at the time.

The *Andrea Doria* cost $29 million to build. In addition to its elegance, the ship was equipped with watertight doors designed to keep major sections of the ship dry, even if parts of the vessel became flooded. The latest radio equipment, an automatic sprinkler system, and two **radar** screens were also installed. In addition, the *Andrea Doria* carried sixteen aluminum lifeboats that could hold two thousand people, more than the total number ever booked on the ship. Perhaps that was why the *Andrea Doria*'s story shocked the world.

The Passengers

On July 25, 1956, the *Andrea Doria* was nearing the U.S. coast on its way to New York City, as it ended its fifty-first round-trip voyage across the Atlantic. The fog was unusually heavy that night, and by 9:00 P.M. it was nearly impossible to see. Alerted of the weather conditions by his crew, Captain Piero Calamai sounded the *Andrea Doria*'s foghorn at regular intervals to warn any ships in the area of their approach. The ship's two radar screens were also diligently checked to ensure that they were working properly. Calamai, the only captain the *Andrea Doria* ever had, took pride in the ocean liner's fine record at sea and hoped to maintain it.

A number of particularly interesting and distinguished passengers were aboard the *Andrea Doria* at the time. They included the beautiful, thirty-two-year-old, dark-haired movie star Ruth Roman, who had acted in more than twenty motion pictures. Ms. Roman was traveling with her four-year-old son and the young boy's nanny. On the last night of the trip, the actress had stayed up dancing in the ballroom with a group of friends. Meanwhile, her son slept soundly in his cabin as his nanny watched over him.

Another young person on the *Andrea Doria* was fourteen-year-old Linda Morgan. Her father (who was not on board) was the well-known news broadcaster Edward P. Morgan. She was accompanied on the *Andrea Doria* by her mother, Jane, her stepfather (New York *Times* reporter Camille Cianfarra), and her eight-year-old half-sister, Joan. Linda's stepfather had made an earlier reservation on another Italian ocean liner, but the family's return was delayed for business reasons.

Still, another young passenger aboard the ship was thirteen-year-old Peter Thieriot. His parents had taken him on this trip as a gift for graduating from grammar school. The family had originally planned to return home by plane, but Peter's mother convinced his father that a leisurely sea voyage would be more fun.

Captain Calamai

Captain Piero Calamai was the son of magazine editor and publisher Oreste Calamai. Piero began his career at sea at the age of eighteen, when he enlisted in the Italian navy as an officer cadet. Captain Calamai had been the youngest captain among the Italian liners. Following the *Andrea Doria* disaster, he went on to command the *Cristoforo Colombo*.

Peter enjoyed the vacation, having made friends with other teens aboard the *Andrea Doria*. After saying goodnight on that final night of the voyage, Peter and his parents went to their cabins. The boy's room was away from his parents' because adjoining rooms had been unavailable. None of them ever imagined that the 50 or so feet separating their cabins could mean the difference between life and death.

Beware of the Fog!

The *Andrea Doria* was not alone at sea that fateful night. Another ship that would affect the fate of many passengers aboard the *Andrea Doria*, was rapidly approaching the ship head-on. Hidden by the fog, the *Stockholm*, a small Swedish-American ship bound for Europe, had begun to enter the

The SS Stockholm

Andrea Doria's path. At about 10:40 P.M., officers on the *Andrea Doria* spotted the *Stockholm* as a small blip on its radar screen. They believed that the *Stockholm* would understand its dangerous course and turn to avoid a collision.

At 11:10 P.M., the steel-reinforced **bow** of the *Stockholm* plowed into the *Andrea Doria*'s side, creating a gaping hole. Fifteen-year-old Martin Sejda had just finished walking around the deck and was about to join his parents in the ballroom when he was startled by what he saw in the water. It was the *Stockholm*, just about to hit the *Andrea Doria*. "I saw her

Several crewmen from the Stockholm *were killed in the bow of the ship.*

lights about three seconds before the crash. The ship was coming in at an angle like it was trying to keep from hitting us," he recalled.

The Collision

At its broadest point, the gash in the *Andrea Doria* was about 40 feet (12.2 m) wide. The *Stockholm* reversed engines and immediately pulled away from the *Andrea Doria*, but the two ships bumped violently, creating several more holes in the *Andrea Doria*'s side. Almost immediately, water flooded the ship. Regrettably, the accident took its toll in human lives.

The violent collision created instant horror on the *Andrea Doria*. Peter Thieriot awoke to the sound of shattering glass and a loud noise outside his cabin. Peter tried to find his parents, but the passageway to their room had been flattened in the crash. They were killed on impact.

Camille Cianfarra died instantly. His wife, Jane Cianfarra, narrowly escaped being crushed to death and was rescued after being trapped in the ship's debris. Her daughter, Linda Morgan, was missing. The girl had been asleep in her cabin when the accident occurred. Her sister Joan, who had been sleeping in the lower bunk, was instantly killed, but fate was kinder to Linda. The *Stockholm's* bow crushed her bed, lifting her up on her mattress and gently dropping her onto the *Stockholm*. She was reported missing for two days before being located by her father in a New York hospital. Morgan phoned Linda's mother, Jane who was recovering at another medical center. Mrs. Cianfarra, still thinking both her daughters were dead, was shocked to hear her former husband say, "Something's happened that some people call a miracle . . . and I'm with her now."

Actress Ruth Roman recalled that she had been dancing in the ballroom when she "heard a big explosion like a firecracker." Although she saw smoke coming from the area of her cabin, she was relieved to find her young son safe and still asleep in his bed. So as not to frighten him, Ms. Roman and the boy's nanny woke the child and told him, "We are going on a picnic."

Once the boy was dressed and in his life jacket, the actress handed the child to a seaman who lowered him into a lifeboat. But just as Ms. Roman started down the ladder to join him, her son's lifeboat pulled away. She shouted for it to wait, but her cries went unheard in the **commotion**. Fortunately, she was put on the next lifeboat and later reunited with her son.

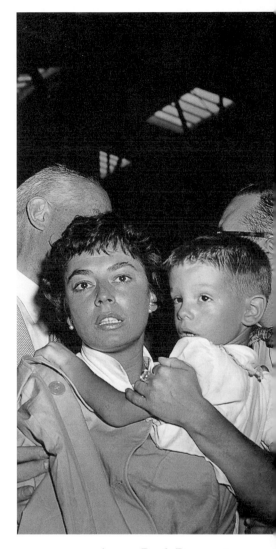

Actress Ruth Roman is reunited with her son Richard.

The Ill-Fated Vessel

At 11:20 P.M., the *Andrea Doria* sent out an SOS, "Need immediate assistance." The *Stockholm*, despite its condition, managed to pull 753 passengers to safety. At 12:45 A.M., the freighter *Cape Ann* arrived. At 1:23 A.M., the *William H. Thomas* arrived, and at 2:00 A.M., the *Ile de France* finally

Survivors of the Andrea Doria arrive in New York aboard the Ile de France.

arrived with desperately needed lifeboats. The waiting *Andrea Doria* passengers broke into cheers at the sight of the massive rescue ship. The all-night rescue operation saved 1,663 people, but 51 lives, including 5 crewmen from the *Stockholm*, were lost at sea. By the next morning, the abandoned *Andrea Doria* had settled to the bottom of the Atlantic Ocean.

In court, the companies that owned the *Andrea Doria* and the *Stockholm* each claimed that the other vessel had been at fault in the accident. The two sides gave different stories in describing the events leading up to the crash, and the incident

The *Stockholm*

was never fully resolved. At times, the accident has been described as the "collision that should never have occurred." Some say that at the last minute, while attempting to avoid an accident, both vessels altered their courses in a way that actually caused the crash.

Decades after the *Andrea Doria* sank, people continue to be fascinated by what took place that foggy night. More than one hundred divers have combed the ship's wreckage beneath the sea. Numerous photos have been taken of its ruins, and on one diving expedition a suitcase was found and returned to a surviving passenger. Yet, there are those who believe that the *Andrea Doria* continues to carry a curse: at least twelve divers have died while exploring the sunken ship.

Hundreds of feet beneath the Atlantic Ocean, a diver gathers china from the Andrea Doria's *dining room.*

Timeline of Maritime Disasters

1854	A British steamer, *City of Glasgow*, is reported missing in the North Atlantic—480 dead
1865	The Mississippi steamer *Sultana* explodes on the Mississippi River in Memphis, Tennessee, killing 1,450 people
1872	After having been reported as missing while sailing from New York to Genoa, the *Mary Celeste* is later found abandoned—loss of life remains unknown
1878	The British steamer *Princess Alice* sinks after a collision in the Thames River, England, killing 250 passengers
1898	Five hundred and forty-nine passengers are killed after a French steamer, *La Bourgogne,* collides with a British sailing ship, *Cromartyshire*, off of Nova Scotia
1904	During an excursion, the *General Slocum* burns in the East River of New York City, killing 1,030 passengers
1912	The infamous British White Star steamer, *Titanic*, hits an iceberg in the North Atlantic and sinks—killing more than 1,500 passengers
1914	The *Empress of Ireland* sinks after a collision with a Norwegian collier in the St. Lawrence River—1,014 dead
1915	The *Lusitania* is torpedoed and sunk by a German submarine off the coast of Ireland, killing 1,198 passengers and crew
1916	More than three thousand people are killed, making it the worst maritime disaster to date, when the French cruiser *Provence* sinks in the Mediterranean

1934	One hundred and thirty-four people die after a fire breaks out aboard the *Morro Castle* off of Asbury Park, New Jersey
1942	The British cruiser *Curaco* sinks after colliding with the *Queen Mary*—338 dead
1948	Six thousand people are killed when a Chinese army evacuation ship explodes off of southern Manchuria, China
1956	The *Andrea Doria* and the *Stockholm* collide off of Nantucket, Massachusetts, killing fifty-one people
1969	A United States destroyer, *Evans*, is split in two by an Australian carrier *Melbourne*, in the South China Sea killing seventy-four crew members
1979	Twenty-three yachts competing in a yacht race in the South Irish Sea, sink or are abandoned after a storm hits, killing eighteen passengers
1987	A ferry from the Phillipines, *Dona Paz*, and an oil tanker collide in the Tablas Strait —4,341 lives are lost
1989	An explosion in the gun turret aboard the *USS Iowa* kills forty-seven crew members
1994	More than one thousand people are killed aboard the passenger ferry *Estonia* when water enters through the bow door
1996	In Lake Victoria, Africa, five hundred lives are lost at sea when the passenger ferry *Bukoba* sinks
1997	A Haitian ferry, *Pride of la Gonâve,* sinks off the coast of Montrouis, Haiti, killing more than two hundred
1998	A passenger boat capsizes off the coast of Nigeria killing 280 people

Glossary

artifact—an object made or changed by humans; an object remaining from a particular period

bow—the forward part of a ship

capacity—the potential or suitability for holding, storing, or accommodating

casualties—people who die or are seriously hurt in some type of accident

catastrophic—the effect of a sudden disaster or serious mishap

commotion—a disturbance, often involving loud noise

distress—a state of danger or desperate need

drill—a physical exercise aimed at perfecting facility and skill

embargo—a government action prohibiting ships from entering or leaving a country's port

evacuate—to move away from an area

fiber-optic—a bundle of thin glass or plastic tubes, through which light passes

hull—the frame or body of a ship

immigrant—a person who comes to a country to take up permanent residence

knots—a unit for measuring the speed of a ship, equal to 6,076 feet (1,852 m) per hour

lifeboats—a strong boat usually carried on a larger ship that is used to save lives during an emergency

negligence—carelessness; not paying proper attention to a particular situation or condition

purser—the ship officer who handles accounts and finances aboard a vessel

radar—a device used to find solid objects by reflecting radio waves off them and by receiving the reflected waves

run aground—a ship that is stuck on the bottom in shallow water

shrapnel—small pieces of metal scattered by an exploding shell or bomb

sonar—an instrument that is used to calculate how deep the water is or where underwater objects are

steerage—a section of accommodations in a passenger ship for those paying the lowest fares

suite—a number of connected rooms in a hotel or on a ship

telegraph—a device or system for sending messages over long distances

transatlantic—crossing or extending across the Atlantic Ocean

water line—the point on the hull of a ship to which the water rises

watertight compartments—an enclosed space that is completely sealed so that water cannot enter it

wireless—a system of communication without wires

To Find Out More

Books

Ballard, Robert D. *Exploring the Titanic.* New York: Scholastic, 1988.

Ballard, Robert D. *The Lost Wreck of Isis.* New York: Scholastic, 1990.

Cohen, Daniel. *Ghosts of the Deep.* New York: Putnam, 1993.

Geography Dept. Runestone Press. *Sunk! Exploring Underwater Archeology.* Minneapolis: Runestone Press, 1994.

Hackwell, W. John. *Diving to the Past: Recovering Ancient Wrecks.* New York: Scribners, 1988.

Nottridge, Rhoda. *Sea Disasters*. New York: Thomson Learning, 1993.

Simon, Seymour. *Icebergs and Glaciers*. New York: Morrow, 1987.

Tanaka, Shelley. *On Board the Titanic: What It Was Like When the Giant Liner Sank*. New York: Hyperion Books for Children, 1996.

Videos

Collision of the Andrea Doria. Southport Video, 1995.

Last Voyage of the Lusitania. National Geographic Video, 1997.

Secrets of the Titanic. National Geographic Video, 1986.

Online Sites and Organizations

Andrea Doria: Tragedy and Rescue at Sea
http://www.andreadoria.org/
Maintained by a survivor of the *Andrea Doria*, this interesting site provides the full history of the luxury ship, including photos, survivors' stories, names of the officers on board that infamous night, and much more.

Encyclopedia Titanica

http://www.rmplc.co.uk/eduweb/sites/phind/

Everything you wanted to know about the *Titanic* can be found at this website. Loaded with facts from passenger and crew lists, to deck plans, lifeboats, and more, this site has it all.

National Disasters of the United States

http://www.usgennet.org/~alhndean/disaster.html

Maintained by the American Local History Network, this site provides an online timeline of some of the most infamous disasters in history, including aeronautical disasters, natural disasters, maritime disasters, and much more!

RMS *Lusitania*

http://members.aol.com/LouAtBuff/Lusitania.html

This site provides statistics and a vivid history of the *Lusitania*, photos of the *Lusitania* and other famous ships, and a variety of links to other websites about the RMS.

United States Coast Guard Home Page

http://www.uscg.mil/welcome.html

Get all the facts and history of the United States Coast Guard at this website. Filled with the latest news and events from the Coast Guard, including helpful boating safety tips, and information about marine safety and environmental protection.

A Note on Sources

In writing on sea disasters, a number of different resources were used. Among the books were *The Great International Disaster*, by James Cornell; *Man Made Catastrophes*, by Lee Davis; *Titanic: Destination Destiny*, by John P. Eaton and Charles A. Haas; *Titanic: An Illustrated History*, by Don Lynch; *Chronicle of the World*, edited by Jerome Burne; *The Morro Castle: Tragedy at Sea*, by Hal Burton; *SAVED!: The Story of the Andrea Doria*, by William Hoffer; *The Greatest Sea Rescue In History*, by William Hoffer; *Eyewitness to Disaster*, by Dan Perkes; and *Great Disasters*, by Karri Ward.

Newspapers and magazines I consulted included *National Geographic* and *The New York Times*. Additional data I found helpful were supplicd by thc U.S. Coast Guard.

—*Elaine Landau*

Index

Numbers in *italics* indicate illustrations.

Allison, Bess, 14

Allison, Helen Lorraine, 14

Allison, Hudson, 14

Andrea Doria, *42*, 43–51, *51*, 53

Artifacts, *20*, *51*

Asbury Park, New Jersey, 40–41, *41*

Astor, John Jacob, 14

Athenai, 10

Atlantic Ocean, 10, 19, 50

Beesley, Laurence, 11

Bryan, William Jennings, 29

Calamai, Oreste, 45

Calamai, Piero, 44, 45, *45*

Californian, 17–18

Cape Ann, 49

Carpathia, 17, *18–19*

Christoforo Colombo, 45

Churchill, Winston, 30, *30*

Cianfarra, Camille, 45, 48

Cianfarra, Jane, 45, 48–49

Cianfarra, Joan, 45, 48

Coast Guard, 39, 40

Cochrane, Charles, 38

Columbus, Christopher, 44

Cruise ships, 34, *34*

Cuba, 33, 35

Cushing, 29

DiCaprio, Leonardo, *21*

Distress signals, 17–18, 19, 37, 38. *See also* SOS signals

Doria, Andrea, 44

Duff-Gordon, Cosmo, 11

Duff-Gordon, Lucille, 11, *11*

England, 7, 23, 28–31

Falaba, 29
Fire, 34, 36–41, *36*
Fleet, Frederick, 10
Fog, 44, 46–48, 51

Germany, 23, 24, 28–30
Global Maritime Distress
    and Safety System, 37
Guggenheim, Benjamin, 16
Gulflight, 29

Icebergs, 10–11, *15*, 19, 21
Ile de France, 49–50, *50*
International Ice Patrol, 19

Juno, 29

Lifeboats, 8, 9, 12, *13*, 14,
    15, 16, 17, 19, 25, 26,
    26–27, 38, 40, 44, 49, 50
Lightoller, Charles Herbert,
    17
Liverpool, England, 23
Lusitania, 22–23, 23–31,
    26–27, *31*, 52

Mato, Antonio, 39
Meisser, Mrs. Robert O., 40
Merchant Marine Act, 36
Mesaba, 10

Morgan, Edward P., 45,
    48–49
Morgan, Linda, 45, 48–49
Morro Castle, *32*, 33–41, *36*,
    41, 52
Morse code, 37
Murdoch, William
    McMaster, 12

New York, 7, 23, 33, 35, 37,
    44, 48, *50*

Prohibition, 33

Radar, 44, 47
Radios, 18, 19, 37–38, 43, 47
Radio Telegraphic
    Conference, 37
Rogers, George White, 38,
    39
Roman, Richard, 44, 49, *49*
Roman, Ruth, 44, 49, *49*
Roosevelt, Theodore, 30
Rostron, Arthur, 17
Royal National Lifeboat
    Institution, 26

Schwieger, Walter, 24–25,
    25, 26, 30
Sejda, Martin, 47

Smith, Edward J., 10, *10*, 14, 19

Sonar technology, 21

SOS signals, 19, 37, 38, 39, 40, 49. *See also* Distress signals

Southampton, England, 7, *9*

Stockholm, S.S., *4*, 46–51, *46*, *47*, 53

Telegraph, 10

Thieriot, Peter, 45–46, 48

Thrasher, Leon C., 29

Titanic, 7–21, *7*, *8–9*, *13*, *15*, 52

Titanic (film), 21, *21*

Titanic (play), 21

Torpedoes, 24–25, 29

Underwater explorations, 21, 51, *51*

United Nations, 37

Vanderbilt, Alfred G., 25–26

Wallace, James Stuart, 11

Ward Line, 40

Warms, William F., 35–36, 37–38, *38*

White Star Line, 7, 12, 18–19, 52

William H. Thomas, 49

Wilmott, Robert, 35, *35*

Wilson, Woodrow, 28, *28*, 29

Winslet, Kate, *21*

World War I, 23, 30

About the Author

Popular author Elaine Landau worked as a newspaper reporter and editor, and as a youth services librarian, before becoming a full-time writer. She has written more than one hundred nonfiction books for young people. Included among her many books for Franklin Watts are the other Watts Library titles on disasters: *Air Crashes*, *Fires*, and *Space Disasters*. Ms. Landau, who has a bachelor's degree in English and journalism from New York University and a master's degree in library and information science from Pratt Institute, lives in Miami, Florida, with her husband and son.